Lincoln Public Library

December 1985

779

Robert Capa

Photographs

Robert Capa

Photographs

Edited by Cornell Capa and Richard Whelan

Alfred A. Knopf   New York   1985

Grateful acknowledgment is made to the following
for permission to reprint previously published material:
Julian Bach Literary Agency, Inc.:
Excerpt from Edward Steichen's eulogy at the funeral of Robert Capa.
Reprinted by permission of Joanna T. Steichen.
Ziff-Davis Publishing Company:
Quote from "Robert Capa: A Memorial Portfolio" by John Steinbeck.
Originally appeared in the September 1954 issue of *Popular Photography*.
Reprinted by permission of Ziff-Davis Publishing Company.

Library of Congress Cataloging in Publication Data
Capa, Robert, 1913–1954.
  Photographs.
  1. Photography, Journalistic. 2. Capa, Robert,
1913–1954. I. Whelan, Richard. II. Capa, Cornell.
III. Title.
TR820.C349 1985   779'.092'4   85-40213
ISBN 0-394-54421-8

Manufactured in the United States of America
First Edition

Frontispiece Photograph by George Rodger

A Note on the Type
The text of this book was set in Gill Sans,
one of the type faces designed by
the celebrated British sculptor Eric Gill (1882–1940)
and first released for use in 1928.

Composed by Ultracomp, New York, New York
Printed in Stonetone by Rapoport Printing Corp.,
New York, New York
Bound by A. Horowitz & Sons, Fairfield, New Jersey
Designed by Arnold Skolnick

Acknowledgments

From among the many people who contributed to the making of this book, we would like to give special thanks to the following: Robert Gottlieb, who is as brilliant, as demanding, and as enthusiastic an editor of pictures as he is of prose; Arnold Skolnick, who not only did a superb job of designing the book but also worked closely with us in selecting the photographs to be included; Ellen McNeilly, who, with a perfectionism and personal dedication unparalleled in publishing, oversaw all aspects of production; Melanie Jackson, our agent, who resolved innumerable problems with wisdom and patience; Eve Arnold, who first led us to Knopf and Bob Gottlieb; Anna Winand, Hiroji Kubota, and Robert Kirschenbaum, who worked with us on the Matsuya department store exhibition and catalogue of Robert Capa photographs that circulated in Japan during 1984; Jimmy Fox and Patricia Strathern of Magnum, Paris, and John Hillelson, London, who, on behalf of the Estate of Robert Capa, recovered many vintage prints from the files of European magazines and photo agencies; Doris O'Neil, who graciously made the files of the Life Picture Service available to us; Philip Pocock, who made copy negatives that often, miraculously, reveal more detail than the vintage prints from which he was working; Cheung Ching Ming, who not only made beautiful new prints from many original and copy negatives but also assisted us immeasurably in readying the book for production; Igor Bakht, Kenneth Siegel, and Robert Glick, who made many additional prints; and Lori Shephard, who generously contributed the two unique vintage prints of Welsh miners to the permanent collection of the International Center of Photography.

But our most special thanks are reserved for Edie Capa, who has worked with Robert Capa's negatives for thirty years and who not only handled our ceaseless requests with great patience and supreme efficiency but also gave us advice, criticism, and encouragement.

An exhibition based on this book has been organized and circulated by the International Center of Photography, New York. We wish to thank all members of the ICP staff, and especially Miles Barth, Ann Doherty, Willis Hartshorn, Anne Hoy, Phyllis Levine, and Art Presson.

We also wish to express our thanks to Alfred A. Knopf, Inc., and in particular to Nancy Clements, Cherie Gillette, Martha Kaplan, Carol Janeway, Jack Lynch, Mary Maguire, and Nina Salter.

Finally, acknowledgment is due to the many editors with whom Robert Capa collaborated closely during his career, and to the staff of Magnum Photos, Inc., New York and Paris. We are especially grateful to Time Inc. and the editors of *Life* for their cooperation.

C.C. & R.W.

TO OUR MOTHER, JULIA
C.C.

Foreword by Cornell Capa

This is the first book that presents the full range of my brother's work. Bob himself produced four heat-of-the-battle titles—first, *Death in the Making* (1938), during the Spanish Civil War; followed by *The Battle of Waterloo Road*, during the London Blitz (1941); then *Slightly Out of Focus* (1947), with his own self-mocking text and illustrative photographs, a serio-comic account of the Second World War, an event so overwhelming he refused to treat it seriously; and finally, *Report on Israel* (1950), a record of the early struggles of that newborn ancient nation.

These four books give an excellent clue to Robert Capa's character as a photographer, a reporter and a passionate human being who was a keenly observant participant in the events around him. During his working life of twenty-two years he eyewitnessed cataclysmic world events. He gave himself the assignment to report on man's self-created inferno, war. For him, luck ran out in Indochina on May 25, 1954, when he stepped on a mine and his role as witness terminated.

My role has been clear: during Bob's lifetime I shared in his life and work; after his death, I dedicated my efforts to having his work seen, understood and appreciated. The first attempt to present a retrospective of his words and photographs was *Images of War*, published in 1964. Since then there have been several exhibitions and catalogs of Bob's work, but no major monographs. Richard Whelan, my collaborator on this book and Bob's biographer, has spent prodigious energy and time to piece together the historical settings and sequences. Bringing these insights to bear, we have together gone through all of Bob's photographs and made a selection that gives a fresh view of the man, his work and the events he covered.

The travails of the decades he witnessed were tragic, but what gave him strength was his sense of humor and irony, a self-deprecating attitude toward his own courage. These were the essential ingredients of the man, the photographer and his self-assumed mission. After D-Day, June 6, 1944, he wrote:

> The war correspondent has his stake—his life—in his own hands, and he can put it on this horse or that horse, or he can put it back in his pocket at the very last minute. I am a gambler. I decided to go in with Company E in the first wave.

In making that decision he was following the advice he often gave to his fellow photographers: "If your pictures aren't good enough, you're not close enough." But behind the humor and the irony and the bravery lay great sensitivity, which led him to remark, with characteristic understatement, "It's not easy always to stand aside and be unable to do anything except to record the sufferings around one."

Bob's compassion was for all sufferers in war, and his photographs captured not only the crucial moments in these events, but also the hearts and imaginations of those who have viewed his work. His life is a testament to difficulty overcome, a challenge met, a gamble won except at the end. Born without means to travel, with a language not useful beyond the borders of a small country, Hungary, he managed to experience the world through a universal means of communication, photography. He was thus able to speak to us all, then and now.

He never thought about his photographs as art. It was not the concern of the time. He was proud of his good pictures, photographs that captured the mood, the moment, photographs that reflected what he saw and felt.

During his short time on earth he lived and loved a great deal. He was born without money, and he died the same. What he left behind is the story of his unique voyage and a visual testimony affirming his own faith in humankind's capacity to endure and occasionally to overcome.

Introduction by Richard Whelan

In December 1938, by which time the twenty-five-year-old Robert Capa had spent just over two years covering the wars in Spain and China, the British magazine *Picture Post* ran an eleven-page layout of his latest battle pictures and prefaced it with a full-page photograph of Capa himself, under which ran the caption "The Greatest War-Photographer in the World: Robert Capa."

The label stuck, and Capa—who went on to cover World War II, the Israeli War for Independence, and the French Indochina War—is still generally thought of simply as a war photographer, though of the approximately 260 images that the editors of the present book have selected as Capa's strongest and most memorable, only about 40 were actually shot in the heat of battle. (It is hardly surprising that their impact is so great despite their relatively small number, for they are among the most intense and immediate shots of battle action ever taken.) Another 120 photographs show people on the periphery of battle: soldiers relaxing behind the lines or preparing to go into combat, refugees whose homes have been destroyed, civilians fleeing before the advance of enemy troops or running for shelter as air-raid alarms sound. But in addition to those 160 images of war are 100 images of peace, albeit sometimes a troubled one—pictures of Parisian street life and political demonstrations, of American junkets and striptease joints, of Israeli immigrants, of children in postwar Japan, and of some of Capa's famous friends: Ernest Hemingway, Pablo Picasso, Gary Cooper, Ingrid Bergman.

The common denominator of the photographs in this book is not war but people—and Capa's extraordinary sensitivity to and sympathy for the human condition. (Asked by a camera-magazine writer for some advice to pass on to amateur photographers, Capa replied that they should "like people and let them know it.") There is only one photograph in this book in which no people, living or dead, are present (pages 60–61), and in that photograph—which shows the interior of a bomb-devastated Madrid apartment—it is their very absence, rendered all the more poignant by what is presumably a family portrait on the wall, that haunts us.

The proportional representation of the three major categories of Capa's work—images of battle, images of the effects of war on individual soldiers and civilians, and images of peace—as well as the almost total absence of photographs that do not deal directly with people, reflects not the editors' biases but the nature of Capa's lifework as it is to be seen on his contact sheets.

As a photographer of people, Capa has much more in common with his friends André Kertész and Henri Cartier-Bresson than has generally been recognized. Indeed, there are a few photographs in this book—those of Parisian children (pages 14–16), that of a Bruges priest conferring with another man about his camera (page 100), that of the Bar des Amis in Marseilles (pages 102–103), that of a Moscow fashion show (page 209), to mention several—that could easily be mistaken for the work of Kertesz or Cartier-Bresson.

Kertész, of course, was one of the great pioneers of 35mm photography, and his example taught Capa much about the Leica's potential for capturing the spirit of a moment with a sense of intimacy and immediacy. Beyond mastery of the small camera, however, there is a more subtle affinity between the two photographers' work. In Capa's images, as in many of Kertész's, one senses the photographer's warm feelings for his subjects and a great gentleness of spirit.

In Paris in the early 1930s, Capa and Cartier-Bresson both came under Kertész's influence and, together with their friend David Seymour ("Chim"), developed a photographic style that sought to capture what Cartier-Bresson called "the decisive moment," a style that later became associated with Magnum Photos, the photographers' cooperative agency that Capa, Cartier-Bresson, Seymour, and a few others founded in 1947. But although Capa's work tends to look more like Cartier-Bresson's than like Kertész's, the resemblance is largely superficial, for by temperament Capa differed radically from Cartier-Bresson, a cool and aloof observer whose images reflect his superbly controlled sense of geometry and his penchant for amusing or disturbing—indeed, surrealistic—juxtapositions. Capa photographed not simply as an observer but as a participant. He got to know many of his subjects, for his lack of inhibiting self-consciousness, his warmth and generosity, his enthusiasm, his high spirits, his charm, and his genuine affection for people of all sorts gave him entree almost everywhere and put people at ease. Capa's work is as passionate and as partisan as Cartier-Bresson's is cerebral and disinterested.

While Kertész and Cartier-Bresson have always thought of themselves as artists (indeed, the latter studied painting before he turned to photography), Capa thought of himself primarily as a journalist. As a teenager in Budapest he settled on journalism as the best way to combine his two great interests: literature and politics. Although he was not then particularly interested in photography, he was exposed—through his friend Eva Besnyö and through his artistic and political mentor Lajos Kassák—to the work of the socially concerned photographers of the Hungarian Szociofotó movement, who had been greatly influenced by the American reformer-photographers Jacob Riis and Lewis W. Hine. After he was exiled from Hungary at the age of seventeen for leftist agitation, Capa studied journalism in Berlin. It was only because of his need to earn some money that he turned to photography. Working in the darkroom of the Dephot agency, which represented many of the best photographers working in the new tradition of human-interest photojournalism that would give rise to such magazines as Life and Picture Post, Capa came to know and to be influenced by the work of Felix H. Man, Walter Bosshard, and Harald Lechenperg. Although these men were photojournalists, they did not work in the tradition of newspaper photographers who simply reported events as they took place. The Dephot photographers editorialized in their work and came up with their own ideas for photo-essays, for which they traveled all over the world.

Given the turbulent political situation in the 1930s and Capa's interest in politics—as well as a great personal stake in the outcome of the struggle against fascism—it was entirely natural that he should be drawn to political reportage. And when politics led to war, it was natural too that he should follow through and cover the fighting. His temperament suited him well for war photography; he was brave, he loved the adventure and camaraderie he found at the front, and he was an inveterate gambler—with his life as well as with his money.

Even after he had become recognized as one of the foremost photographers of the century, Capa used to tell his friends, "I'm not a photographer, I'm a journalist," and it seems to have been out of a certain scorn for the artistic pretensions of photography that he adamantly refused to acquire any more photographic technique than absolutely necessary. He never fully mastered the use of flashbulbs; he was often very careless in the darkroom; and some of his editors used to wonder whether he had intentionally built into his camera a device for scratching his film. Perhaps Capa felt that it would be blasphemous to be too concerned with the technical niceties of a picture in which people were shown in danger of their lives and that there would be something obscene in worrying about making a fine print of a picture of human suffering. Diana Forbes-Robertson, with whom Capa collaborated on a book about the London Blitz, recalls that he used to say, "I'd rather have a strong image that is technically bad than vice versa."

And yet it must be said that Capa was, after all, an artist—as is anyone who does his work with passion, intelligence, skill, sensitivity, grace, wit, and force of character.

Capa had a strong innate sense of composition and graphic impact, but he didn't have anything like Cartier-Bresson's horror of cropping. He expected as a matter of course that in laying out his photographs for publication, editors would crop some of them, and many of his own vintage prints present cropped versions of the images on his negatives. In some cases the editors of the present book have chosen to restore images to their original full-frame format. (One example is the photograph of Chinese refugees riding on top of a railroad car [page 95]; the wonderful diminishing perspective that leads the eye into the lower left-hand corner was cropped off in existing vintage prints.) In a few cases, images have been newly cropped to get rid of such extraneous details as heads or hands that intruded into the frame. In short, we have treated Capa's images photojournalistically.

Going through the Capa estate's archives of contact sheets and vintage prints, the editors found in a number of cases variant images stronger than the versions that have been published in the past. Perhaps the most striking example is the photograph that Capa took in the military cemetery in Namdinh (page 237). Although the version that was originally published in *Life* and that has been reprinted ever since was cropped to transform a horizontal image into a vertical one, it still includes on the right a young child who is paying no attention to the two mourning women. The version of the image in the present book is printed almost full-frame from a vertical negative shot a few moments later. In the new version the distracting child has wandered out of range, while the woman with her back to the camera is planting a bundle of sticks on the grave, a gesture of haunting mystery and poignance. To plant the sticks she has bent over, allowing us to see the face of the other grieving woman more clearly. All in all, the new version is considerably more powerful than the old.

There is one variety of variant image that the editors decided not to reproduce in this book: color transparencies. The Kodachrome shots that Capa took of the aftermath of an air raid in Hankow in September 1938 are of historical interest, for they may well be the first color pictures of war ever published. (*Life* devoted two pages to them.) But as images they are not as strong as the related black-and-white photographs, for in them we are aware first and foremost of the distracting novelty of color. That sense of distraction remains characteristic of the relatively few color transparencies that Capa shot for a number of stories throughout the rest of his career, alternating a 35mm camera and a Rolleiflex loaded with black-and-white film and another 35mm camera loaded with color film. In the color pictures he shot in Indochina just before he died, for example, the eye is so overwhelmed by the blue of the sky and the green of the grass that it takes a while to see what is going on. Capa's black-and-white photographs, on the other hand, are like X-ray plates of form, action, and emotion, in which the photographer and his camera have cut through to the heart of the matter.

There is still another kind of variant image that emerges from a study of Capa's work: photographs that strongly recall ones he had made years earlier. Compare, for instance, the photograph of a man holding a boy with a bandaged leg that Capa took in the Spanish hilltop town of Teruel in 1937 (page 62) and the uncannily similar image of a man holding a girl with a bandaged leg that he took in the Sicilian hilltop town of Troina in 1943 (page 134). In this case—as with photographs of Spaniards on the one hand and Chinese on the other watching air battles or running for shelter when air-raid alarms sounded—Capa seems to have been dwelling on the sameness of war wherever it takes place. In other cases of remarkable similarity, however, there seems to have been a certain element of vicarious revenge or of righting some of the terrible wrongs he had witnessed. Thus his photographs of Axis prisoners held by the Allies in camps surrounded with barbed wire countered those he had taken of Spanish Loyalist exiles in similar camps, and his pictures of joyful refugees returning to their homes in Tunis after the Allied victory balanced ones of Spanish refugees fleeing their homes.

Capà was by nature and by profession a storyteller, and his contact sheets present a narrative continuity from which certain pictures—those that capture "decisive moments" and that have been recognized as his masterpieces—stand out. As images, those great pictures are self-sufficient, but as the historical documents that they also are, their decipherment can be aided by restoring them to the contexts of the photo-stories for which they were originally taken. In the case of Capa's great photograph of a shaven-headed *collaboratrice* being led by a jeering crowd through the streets of Chartres (pages 166–167), for instance, study of the picture's context led to the discovery that the young woman is accompanied by her equally shaven-headed mother—whose presence was never noticed, or at least never mentioned, by previous caption writers. Furthermore, several pictures from the story that have hitherto been overshadowed by the famous picture—and have thus been omitted from previous collections of Capa's work—turn out to be extremely powerful in their own right (pages 162–165).

The photographs in this book have been arranged as much as possible in accordance with chronology, though, for instance, it has seemed advisable in the interest of continuity to follow the Spanish Civil War through to its conclusion in 1939 before backtracking to the photographs that Capa took in China in 1938. The layouts and captions emphasize the photojournalistic nature of Capa's work, for this book is intended not only as a collection of extraordinary images taken by a great photographer but also as a record of three of the most eventful decades of the twentieth century as witnessed by a great journalist.

The Photographs

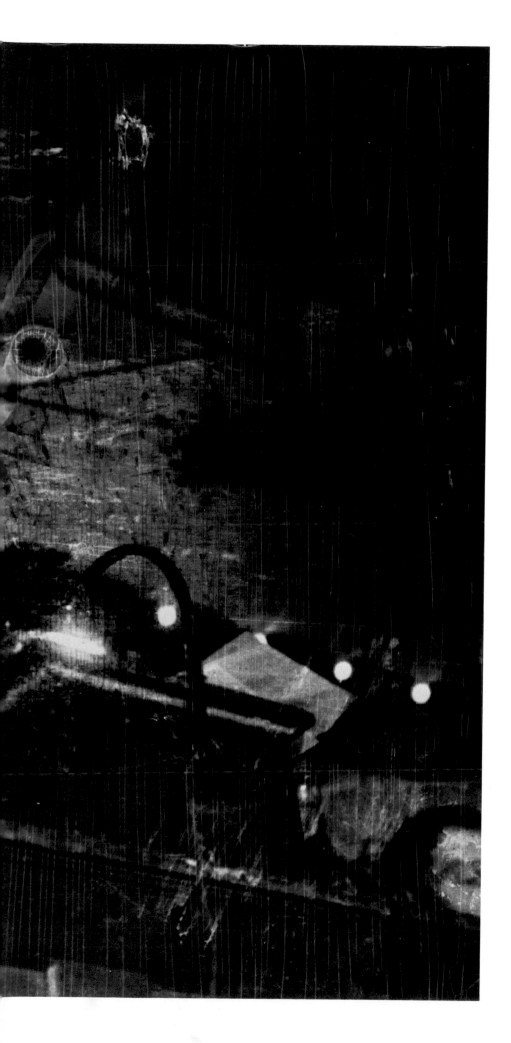

Copenhagen, November 27, 1932. Leon Trotsky
lecturing Danish students on the history of the Russian
revolution. Capa's coverage of Trotsky's speech was his
first published story.

Right: Borinage region, Belgium, November 1937.
Below: Saarbrücken, September 1934. Four
months before the plebiscite that would return the
Saarland to Germany.

Saarland, September 1934.

Above: Paris, spring 1936. Curb traders on the portico of the Bourse.
Right: Seville, April 1935. Spectators at a Holy Week procession.

Opposite above: Verdun, France, July 12, 1936. German delegates at the peace rally held to commemorate the twentieth anniversary of the battle of Verdun.
Opposite below: Geneva, June 30, 1936. When Italian journalists at the League of Nations whistled and catcalled to interrupt Haile Selassie's speech protesting Italy's invasion of Abyssinia, a Spanish journalist was wrongly arrested as one of the agitators. When he continued to protest his innocence, the policemen clapped their hands over his mouth.

Left: Verdun, July 12, 1936.
Below: Paris, May 28, 1939. On the anniversary of the defeat of the 1871 Commune of Paris, French Communists and surviving *communards* gathered in Père-Lachaise Cemetery before the plaque honoring the Commune's dead. Standing in the second row (second, third, and fourth from the left) are party leaders Jacques Duclos, André Marty, and Maurice Thorez.

10   Paris, November 11, 1936.

12

Above: Paris, spring 1936. Couples hoping to break into the movies performing at the Ciné Crochet before a film camera and an audience.
Right: Paris, May 1, 1937.

Paris, c. 1936.

Left: Jardin du Luxembourg, Paris, c. 1936.
Below: Paris, 1936

18

Paris, 1936.

Opposite above: Paris, April 24, 1937. Léon Jouhaux, head of the Confédération Générale du Travail, a socialist labor organization, speaking at a giant rally in the Bois de Vincennes.
Opposite below: Brussels, April 1937. Léon Degrelle, candidate of the fascist-style Rex Party, campaigning for election to the Belgian parliament.
Below: Biarritz, October 22, 1936. At a congress of the Radical-Socialist Party (actually neither radical nor socialist but bourgeois and center-liberal) a deep split was manifested when some members gave the clenched-fist salute of the left-liberal Front Populaire coalition (to which the party belonged) and others the fascist salute.

Left: Paris, April–May 1936.
Above: St.-Denis (Paris), May 3, 1936. National election runoffs.

24

Above: Paris, July 14, 1936. Maurice Thorez (left), head of the French Communist Party, and Roger Salengro, Minister of the Interior, have a word on the reviewing stand of the Bastille Day parade celebrating the Front Populaire victory in the national elections.
Right: Boulogne-Billancourt (Paris), May–June 1936. Renault factory workers.

Boulogne-Billancourt (Paris), May 28, 1936.
Workers asleep in the Renault factory on the first
night of the sit-in strike.

Above right: St.-Ouen (Paris), May–June 1936.
Sit-in strikers at the Lavalette Construction
Company plant sat on the surrounding walls to visit
with their families and friends.
Below right: Paris, c. June 12, 1936. A guard of the
Galeries Lafayette department store on strike.

Paris, c. June 12, 1936. The rooftop
terrace of the Galeries Lafayette
during the strike.

St.-Ouen (Paris), May–June 1936.
Left: Strikers at the Lavalette plant.
Below: A basket of sausages sent to
the Lavalette strikers by a
sympathetic butcher.

Paris, July 14, 1936. Bastille Day parade. The Soviet writer Maxim Gorky, who was revered by the international Communist movement, had died a few weeks earlier.

Barcelona, August 1936.
Departure of troops for the front.

UHP
JURAD SOBRE ESTAS LETRAS HERMAN
ANTES MORIR QUE CONSENTIR TIRANO

Left: Barcelona, August 1936. Women of the Communist militia training on a beach near the city.
Below: Barcelona, August 1936.

Right: Leciñena (Aragón front), August 1936. Men of the ṣemi-Trotskyist POUM (Partido Obrero de Unificación Marxista) militia.
Below: Madrid, November–December 1936.

36

Córdoba front, September 1936.

Near Cerro Muriano (Córdoba front), c. September 5, 1936. The man in the white shirt is the Loyalist soldier who is seen falling in Capa's most famous photograph (overleaf). The initials "CNT" embroidered on his cap stand for Confederación Nacional del Trabajo, an anarcho-syndicalist organization.

Near Cerro Muriano (Córdoba front), c. September 5, 1936.   43

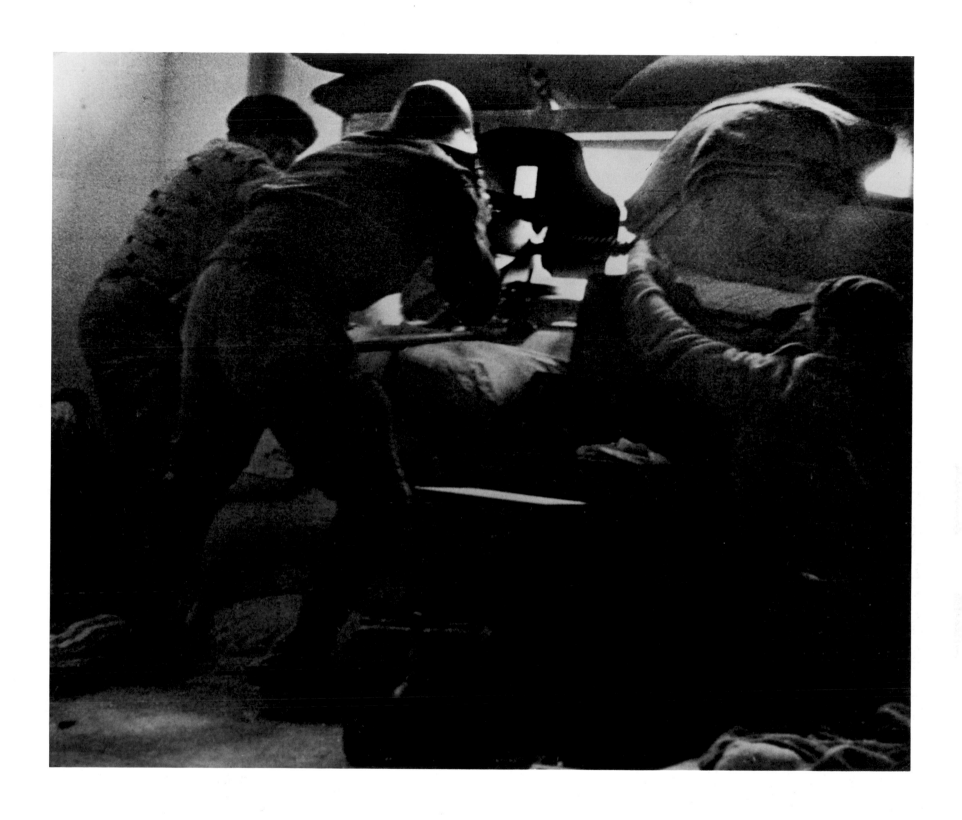

Left: Madrid, November 1936. Men of the International Brigades' Thälmann Battallion in one of the model-farm buildings on the outskirts of the University City.
Above: Madrid, November 1936. Men of the Commune de Paris Battalion in the university's Medical School.

Madrid, November 1936.
Above: In the West Park, south of the University
City, Loyalists manning barricades built with
suitcases that had been taken from the checkroom
of the nearby North Station and filled with dirt.
Right: Near the slaughterhouses outside the city a
wounded man is helped to safety.

Madrid, February 1937. Loyalist earthworks around the Clinical Hospital, one of the principal Insurgent bastions in the University City.

Madrid, November–December 1936.
Behind the lines.

Bilbao, May 1937. Air-raid alarm.

Bilbao, May 1937.

Barcelona, January 1939.

Above: Madrid, November–December 1936. The homeless and others seeking refuge from bombing on the platform of the Gran Vía metro station.
Right: Murcia, February 1937. Refugees from Málaga.

Madrid, November–December 1936

60   Madrid, November–December 1936.

Left: Teruel (Aragón), December 21, 1937.
Above: Teruel, January 3, 1938. Loyalist soldiers
inside the Civil Governor's palace, the last major
bastion of Insurgent resistance in this strategically
located hilltop town. Earlier in the day the
Loyalists had detonated mines to blow away one
entire wall of the palace.

Teruel, December 21–24, 1937.

Near Fraga (Aragón),
November 7, 1938.
Loyalist offensive
along the Río Segre.

Near Fraga, November 7, 1938.

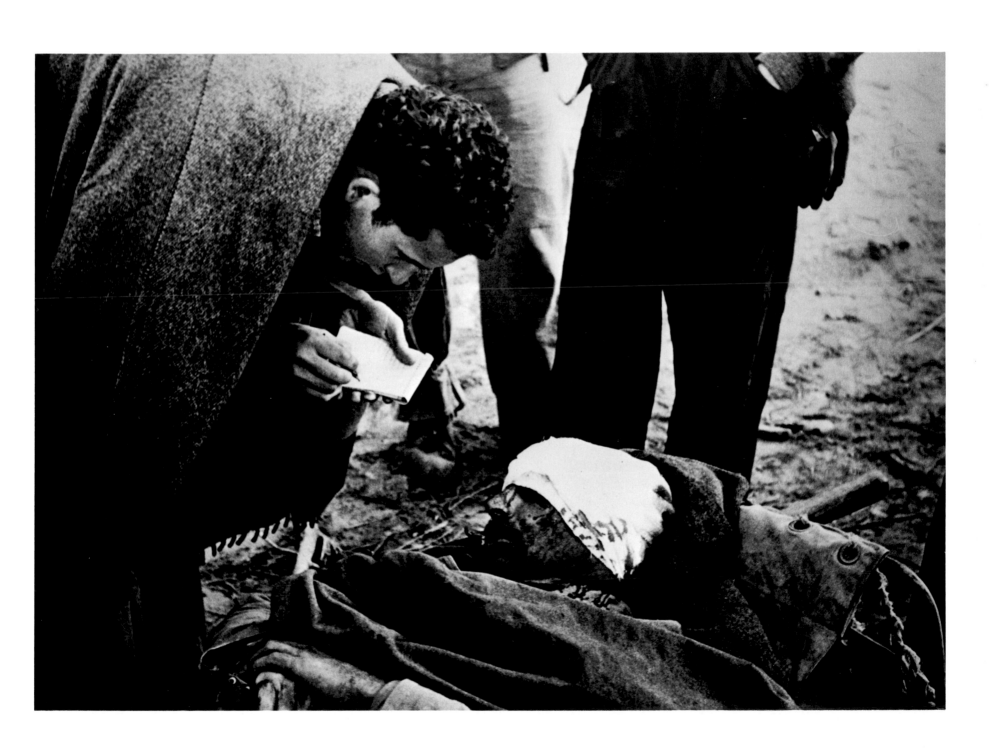

Near Barcelona, October 25, 1938.
Farewell ceremony for the volunteers of
the International Brigades.

Above: On the road from Tarragona to Barcelona, January 15, 1939.
Right: On the road from Barcelona to the French border, January 25–27, 1939.

Barcelona, January 1939. The girl whom Capa photographed in close-up is visible immediately to the right of the curb at the bottom of his picture of the crowd outside a refugee transit center.

Above: Barcelona, January 13, 1939. General mobilization of all men up to the age of fifty.
Right: Argelès-sur-Mer, France, March 1939. Not even close relatives were allowed to enter the camps in which the French government interned the Spanish Loyalist soldiers who had crossed the border into exile after their defeat.

On the beach between Argelès-sur-Mer and Le Barcarès, France, March 1939. Exiled Loyalists being transferred from one internment camp to another.

Above: Hankow, March 12, 1938. Schoolboys at the parade commemorating the thirteenth anniversary of Sun Yat-sen's death and celebrating recent government victories.
Right: Hankow, March 1938.

Hankow, August–September 1938. Chou En-lai, at the time
Mao's liaison with the government of Chiang Kai-shek.

Hankow, July 4, 1938. Chiang Kai-shek
at a meeting of his Supreme War Council.

Above: Taierhchwang (Suchow front), April 7, 1938. Chinese soldier standing guard on the ramparts of the town, taken from the Japanese the previous night.
Right: Taierhchwang, April 1938. Chinese troops marching past the town along the banks of the Grand Canal.

China, April–September 1938.

Below: Taierhchwang, April 1938. Returning to the battle-devastated town.
Right: Hankow, July–September 1938. Air-raid alarm.

Hankow, July–September 1938.

Hankow, July–September 1938.

Left: Taierhchwang, April 1938. All but the most
severely wounded had to walk six miles for a train
to hospitals behind the lines.
Above: Near the Suchow front, April 1938.

Near the Suchow front, April 1938.

Pleyben, Brittany, July 1939. Tour de France.

Opposite above, left: Bruges, Ascension Day (May 18), 1939.
Opposite above, right: Brussels, April–May 1939. Adolphe
Max, Burgomaster of the city for thirty years, speaking to his
dog Happy, the last in a long succession of terriers—all with
the same name.
Opposite below: Bruges, Ascension Day, 1939. Procession of
the Holy Blood.
Above: Antwerp, April–May 1939. The harborside Café
Bernstein.

Left: Marseilles, March 1939.
Above: Paris, September 1939. A French reservist
stopping at a sidewalk café before reporting for duty.

103

Left: Owosso, Michigan, December 1940. Party with a hangover theme.
Above: New York, December 1940. Jinx Falkenburg, then appearing in a minor role in the musical comedy *Hold On to Your Hats*.
Below: New York, November 19, 1939. Dorothy Maynor and Paul Robeson at the party following the soprano's Town Hall debut.

Sun Valley, Idaho, October 1941.
Above: Ernest Hemingway and his son Gregory.
Right: Gary Cooper.

New York, September–October 1937.
Stillman's Gym.

On a train between Memphis, Tennessee, and Hot Springs, Arkansas, March 9, 1940. Memphis political boss Edward Hull Crump took a thousand of his "good friends" on a one-day junket to the races at Hot Springs.

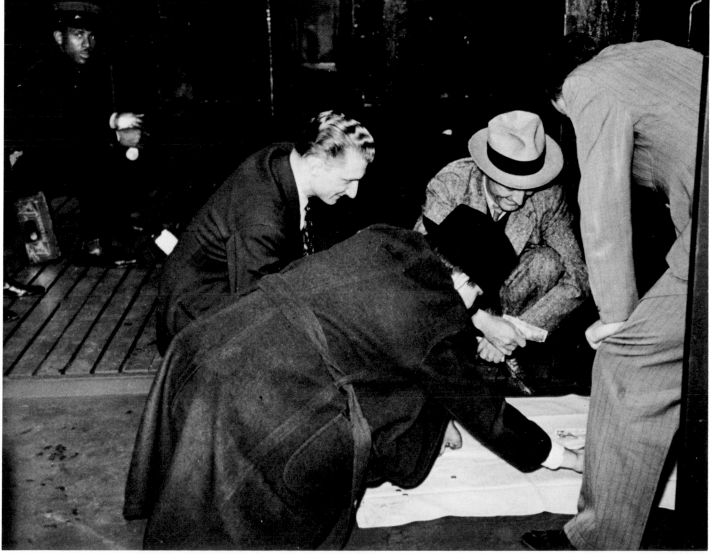

Overleaf: Calumet City, Illinois, December 1940. Steelworkers and boilermakers from Hammond and Gary, just across the Indiana state line, flocked to this "sin city's" 308 nightclubs on Saturday night.

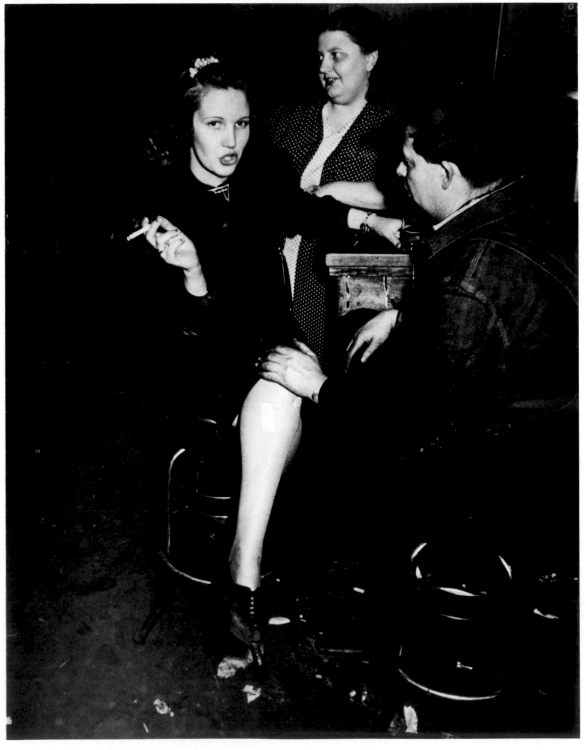

Left: Mexico City, July 7, 1940.
The first fatality in election day violence.
Below: Mexico City, July 9, 1940.

London, June–July 1941.
Left: St. John's Church, Waterloo Road.
Below: Evening tea in an air-raid shelter.

Rhondda Valley, Wales, June 1942. Coal miners.

Below: London, January–February 1943. American soldier with war orphans ''adopted'' by his unit.
Right: London, June–July 1941. Whichcote Street, just off Waterloo Road.

Chelveston, England, November 1942. Men of the U.S. 301st Bomber Group after a daylight mission. The plane's landing gear had been shot away, but the pilot managed to make a successful belly landing.

El Guettar, Tunisia, March 1943.

Maknassy, Tunisia, March 22, 1943.

Tunisia, April 1943. American fighter ace.

Chiunzi Pass, above Maiori,
Sorrento peninsula, Italy,
September 1943. Soldiers relaxing
in front of their foxholes during a
lull in the fighting.

Chiunzi Pass, September 1943.

Maiori, September 19, 1943. Operating
room set up in a church in the northern
sector of the Salerno beachhead.

Below: Along the road to Naples, c. September 30, 1943.
Opposite above: Troina, Sicily, August 6, 1943. The first American patrol entering the town.
Opposite below: Outside Troina, August 4–5, 1943. Reconnaissance mission.

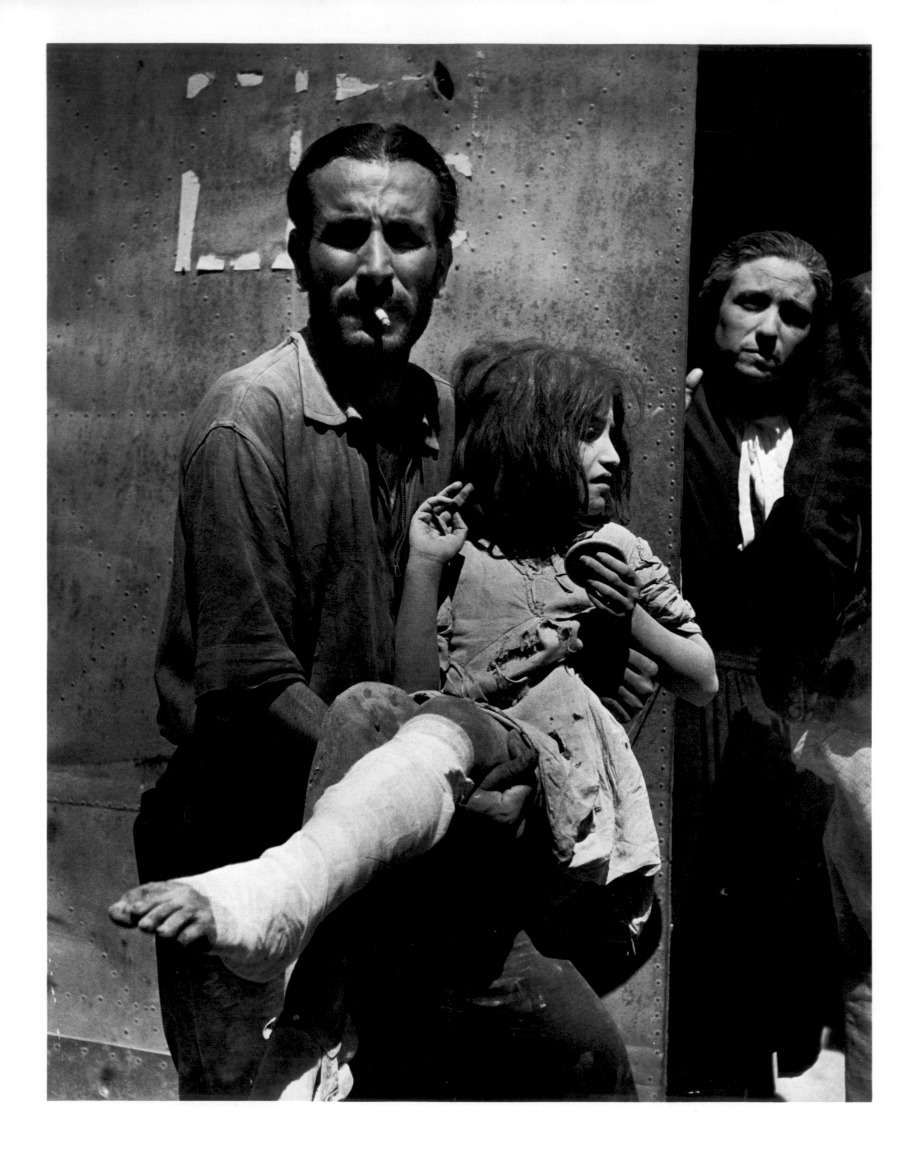

Left: Troina, August 6, 1943.
Above: Radicosa (near Cassino), January 4, 1944.

Below: Along the road to Naples, c. September 30, 1943. A wounded German discovered by American paratroopers in a barn.
Opposite above: Near Nicosia, Sicily, July 28, 1943. German prisoner.
Opposite below: Sicily, July–August 1943.

Left: Mount Pantano (near Cassino), Italy, December 18, 1943.
Right: Moscoso Notch (near Cassino), January 4, 1944.

Naples, October 2, 1943. Funeral of twenty teenaged partisans at the Liceo Sannazaro in the Vómero district. Led by one of their teachers, the boys had fought the Germans during the four days before the Allies entered the city.

Monreale, just outside Palermo, Sicily,
July 22, 1943.

Left: Palermo, Sicily, July 23, 1943.
Below: Agrigento, Sicily, July 17–18, 1943.

Above: Cefalù, Sicily, July 26, 1943. Street scene two days after the town had been liberated.
Right: Near Nicosia, Sicily, July 28, 1943. An Italian soldier straggling behind a column of his captured comrades as they march off to a POW camp.

Omaha Beach, near Colleville-sur-Mer, Normandy coast,
June 6, 1944. American troops landing on D-Day.

Omaha Beach, near Colleville-sur-Mer, Normandy coast,
June 6, 1944. American troops landing on D-Day.

Omaha Beach, June 1944.
Left: The beachhead several days after D-Day.
Above: French fishermen looking at bodies awaiting burial.
Right: Using the hood of a jeep as an altar, a Roman Catholic chaplain says Mass at the inauguration of an American cemetery.

Below: Southwest of St.-Lô, July 26–30, 1944. U.S. 2nd Armored Division.
Opposite: St.-Sauveur-le-Vicomte, south of Cherbourg, June 16, 1944.
U.S. 82nd Airborne Division.

Overleaf left: Near Gavray, Normandy, c. August 1, 1944. Returning to the liberated town.
Overleaf right: Notre-Dame-de-Cenilly, southwest of St.-Lô, July 28, 1944.

Left: Granville, Normandy, July 31, 1944.
Above: Near Chartres, c. August 20, 1944.

160

Opposite above: Cherbourg, June 26, 1944.
Opposite below: Cherbourg, June 27, 1944.
Right: Southwest of St.-Lô, July 26–30, 1944.
Below: St.-Malo, August 9, 1944. A French
prostitute follows her captured German
customers rather than face the wrath of her
compatriots.

Chartres, August 18, 1944.
Above: Just after the Allies liberated the town, a Frenchwoman who had collaborated with the Germans is led into the courtyard of the Préfecture de Police to have her head shaved.
Right: Collaborators.

Chartres, August 18, 1944. The young woman had had a baby by a
German soldier. The older woman is her mother. (In the group
portrait on page 163, they are standing third and fifth from the left.)

Chartres, August 18, 1944. The two women from the preceding photographs being marched home. (The mother is visible over the right shoulder of the man carrying the cloth sack.)

Left: Alençon, August 12, 1944.
Above: Paris, August 25, 1944.

Paris, August 25, 1944. French troops and Resistance fighters flushing the last Germans out of the area between the Invalides and the Palais Bourbon.

Paris, August 26, 1944.
Left: General Charles de Gaulle leading the triumphal
parade down the Avenue des Champs-Elysées.

Paris, August 26, 1944.

Paris, August 26, 1944. When snipers in buildings overlooking the Place de l'Hôtel de Ville opened fire on the triumphal parade, the panicked crowd fell to the pavement.

Paris, August 25–26, 1944.

South of Bastogne, Belgium,
December 23–26, 1944. U.S. infantry
crossing a frozen field
during the Battle of the Bulge.

South of Bastogne, December 23–26, 1944.

184   South of Bastogne, December 23–26, 1944.

Above: Arras, France, March 23, 1945. U.S. paratroopers,
their hair cut Mohawk-style for luck and esprit de corps, are
briefed for the next day's jump across the Rhine.
Right: Near Wesel, Germany, March 24, 1945.

Near Wesel, March 24, 1945.

Leipzig, April 18, 1945.

Leipzig, April 18, 1945. After an American soldier firing his machine gun from an apartment balcony had been shot by a German sniper, the dead man's comrades rushed down to the street and found several German soldiers, one of whom was the sniper, hiding in an abandoned streetcar.

Nuremberg, c. April 20, 1945.
Below: Private Hubert Strickland, who had driven the jeep in
which Capa entered Paris on the day the city was liberated,
mockingly giving a Nazi salute in Hitler's mammoth stadium.

Top: Berlin, September 7, 1945. The first Rosh Hashanah
services to be held in any of the city's synagogues since 1938.
Above: Berlin, August 1945. An American soldier using sign
language to sell a watch to a Russian.
Right: Berlin, August 1945.

Above: Normandy beachhead, June 1944. General
Omar N. Bradley, who had recently had a boil on his
nose lanced.
Right: Hollywood, July–October 1946. Ingrid Bergman
shooting a scene for *Arch of Triumph*.

Above: London, May 1944. Ernest Hemingway in the London Clinic recovering from injuries sustained when the car in which he was riding home from a party given by Capa crashed into a steel water tank.
Right: Golfe-Juan, France, August 1948. Pablo Picasso with his son Claude.

Left: Cimiez (Nice), August 1949. Henri Matisse drawing with a bamboo pole tipped with charcoal.
Above: Golfe-Juan, August 1948. Picasso and Françoise Gilot. In the background is Picasso's nephew, Javier Vilato.

Left: Hollywood, April–May 1946. While shooting *Notorious*, Alfred Hitchcock directs the cameraman to zoom in on the wine-cellar key in Ingrid Bergman's hand.

Below: Independence, Missouri, December 1948. President Harry S Truman, visiting his hometown for Christmas, out on his early-morning constitutional.

Warsaw, October 1948.

208

Above: Ukraine, August 1947.
Right: Moscow, September 1947.

Tel Aviv, June 22, 1948. When extreme right-wing Irgunists tried to unload a shipment of arms during a cease-fire, government troops fired on their ship, the *Altalena*.

Tel Aviv, November 1950. Menachem Begin.

Left: Tel Aviv, May 14, 1948. David Ben-Gurion reading the
proclamation of Israel's statehood.
Below: Tel Aviv, November 14, 1950. Chaim Weizmann, the
first president of Israel, arriving to cast his ballot in the
municipal elections.

214

Haifa, May–June 1949.

Opposite: Haifa, May–June 1949. Immigrants from Turkey.
Left: Rosh Hay'n internment camp, Shaar Aliyah, near Haifa,
October–November 1950.
Below: Near Gedera (south of Tel Aviv), November–
December 1950. In a then-nameless village for blind
immigrants and their families, three men are led toward the
community dining hall.

Above: Tel Aviv, May 1949.
Right: Jerusalem, May–June 1949.
Opposite: Jerusalem, May–June 1949. A meeting of the
Talmud Society in the Mea Shearim district.

Overleaf: Tel Aviv, May 1949. The rusting hulk of the *Altalena*.

Opposite and left: Zürs, Austria, February 1950.
Below: Biarritz, August 1951.

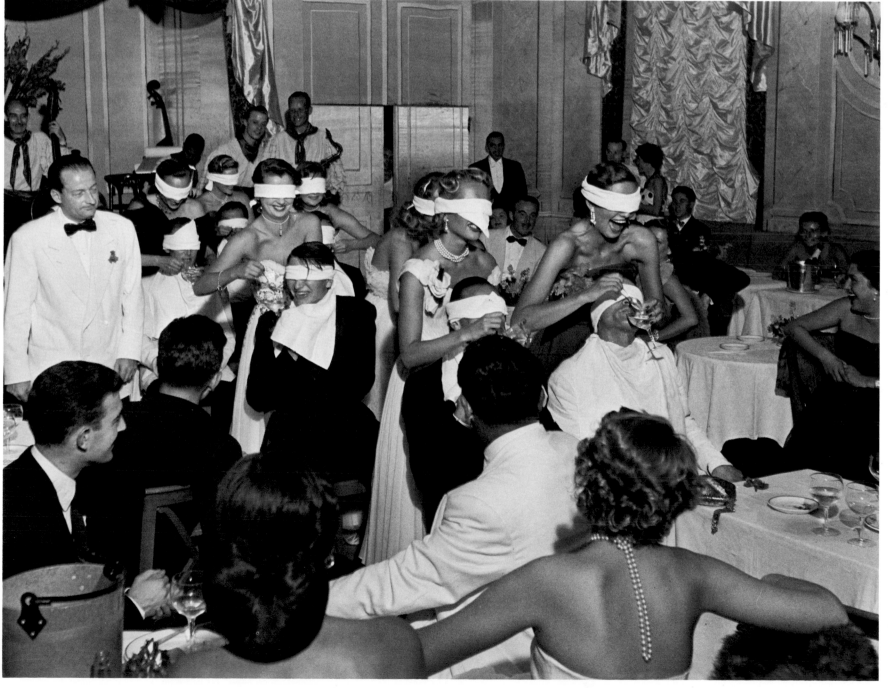

Paris, July 14, 1952. Diners at the Tour d'Argent watching the Bastille Day fireworks.

Japan, April 1954.

Left: Luang Prabang, Laos, c. May 10, 1954. French soldier
after retreat from positions near Dienbienphu, which had
fallen to the Viet Minh on May 7 after a long siege.
Above: West of Namdinh, May 24, 1954.

On the road from Namdinh to Thaibinh,
Red River delta, May 25, 1954.

Below: Along the road to Thaibinh, May 25, 1954.
Right: Namdinh, May 21, 1954.

Along the road to Thaibinh, May 25, 1954. French soldiers advancing toward a Viet Minh mortar position that had the road under fire.

Along the road to Thaibinh, May 25, 1954.
Left: Soldier carrying a mine detector.
Above: The last black-and-white photograph that Robert Capa ever took.
(He took one similar color shot a few seconds after this with his other camera.)
He was killed by a mine while climbing the dike on the right.

Capa knew what to look for and what to do with it when he found it. He knew, for example, that you cannot photograph war, because it is largely an emotion. But he did photograph that emotion by shooting beside it. He could show the horror of a whole people in the face of a child. His camera caught and held emotion.

Capa's work is itself the picture of a great heart and an overwhelming compassion. No one can take his place. No one can take the place of any fine artist, but we are fortunate to have in his pictures the quality of the man.

I worked and traveled with Capa a great deal. He may have had closer friends but he had none who loved him more. It was his pleasure to seem casual and careless about his work. He was not. His pictures are not accidents. The emotion in them did not come by chance. He could photograph motion and gaiety and heartbreak. He could photograph thought. He captured a world, and it was Capa's world.

JOHN STEINBECK

Capa is a dangerous influence because he has perfected the trick of making life among the bombed cities and the stinking battlefields of our time seem gay and dashing and glamorous. His is a career of flight: flight from the dreadful evidence of his own cameras. It is a flight which takes him in many directions, but always, inexorably, in the same style. It is an appealing style, old-fashioned and formalized, and its first and only rule is: remain debonair.

How a poverty-stricken young wanderer through the hideous slums of Europe between the wars could have chosen this ludicrously chivalric motto as his guiding principle, probably not even Capa fully understands. And it is a rigorous and demanding creed to live up to. It means that one must never seem weary, one must always be ready to go to the next bar or the next war, no matter how late the hour or unattractive the war. It means that a man must always sit through every poker pot and call every hand; must lose six months' salary and buy the next round of drinks, lend thoughtlessly and borrow ceremoniously, consort only with very pretty women, preferably those who are mentioned often in the newspapers; it means that one must always know where to buy a bottle, in the dryest town, and what restaurants are serving the best dinners, even in times of famine.

Only in the morning, as he staggers out of bed, does Capa show that the tragedy and sorrow through which he has passed have left their marks on him. His face is gray, his eyes are dull and haunted by the dark dreams of the night; here, at last, is the man whose camera has peered at so much death and so much evil, here is a man despairing and in pain, regretful, not stylish, undebonair. Then Capa drinks down a strong, bubbling draught, shakes himself, experimentally tries on his afternoon smile, discovers that it works, knows once more that he has the strength to climb the glittering hill of the day, dresses, and sets out, nonchalant, carefully light-hearted, to the bar of "21," or the Scribe, or the Dorchester, all places where this homeless man can be at home, where he can find his friends and amuse them and where his friends can help him forget the bitter, lonely, friendless hours of the night behind him and the night ahead.

IRWIN SHAW

Despite all his inventions and postures, Capa has, somewhere at his center, a reality. This is his talent—which is compounded of humaneness, courage, taste, a romantic flair, a callous attitude toward mere technique, an instinct for what is appropriate, and an ability to relax. At the very core, he even has modesty. He has the intuition of a gambler ... [He] has humor. He has a clear idea of what makes a great picture: "It is a cut of the whole event," he says, "which will show more of the real truth of the affair to someone who was not there than the whole scene."

Above all—and this is what shows in his pictures—Capa, who has spent so much energy on inventions for his own person, has deep, human sympathy for men and women trapped in reality.

JOHN HERSEY

He understood life. He lived life intensely. He gave richly of what he had to give to life.... [He] lived valiantly, vigorously, with a rare integrity.

As a photographer we know him with few peers in his field and we must add to this the influence and inspiration he has given to the rest of us.

As one of the elders in the field of photography, I believe I am privileged to speak for his colleagues. I call them to attention: "Robert Capa, we salute you."

EDWARD STEICHEN